EssaySnark's Strategies for the 2014-'15 MBA Application for UC-BERKELEY HAAS

by EssaySnark®

Snarkolicious Press

First edition July 31, 2011

2014 edition published July 4, 2014
version 4.0

Snarkolicious Press
P. O. Box 50021
Palo Alto, CA 94303

www.snarkoliciouspress.com

978-1-938098-26-0

© 2011-2014 by EssaySnark

Cover image © Eric Isselée, used under license from Fotolia.com

All rights reserved. No part of this book may be reproduced or transmitted in any form or by any means, electronic or mechanical, including photocopying, recording, or by an information storage system, without permission from the publisher. Essay questions copyright UC-Berkeley Haas School of Business.

This publication is provided "as is", without warranty of any kind, either express or implied. The author and Snarkolicious Press assume no liability responsibility for errors or omissions in this publication or other documents which are referenced or linked to this publication. While we certainly hope that you will be successful in your quest for admission to an MBA program, we cannot offer any promises that you will be, whether or not you adopt the advice provided herein. In no event shall Snarkolicious Press or its authors, principals, subsidiaries, partners, or owners, be liable for any special, incidental, indirect or consequential damages of any kind, or any damages whatsoever, arising out of or in conjunction with the use or performance of this information. Applicants to any graduate program or university should verify the school's policies, application requirements, processes, procedures, and other criteria. This publication could include technical or other inaccuracies or typographical errors. Changes are periodically added to the information herein; these changes will be incorporated into new editions of this publication. Thus, different versions or formats of this publication may include different information.

Look for other *SnarkStrategies Guides* (digital and paperback) at your favorite bookseller or on the EssaySnark blahg at http://essaysnark.com.

FOLLOW ESSAYSNARK ON TWITTER!

EssaySnark's Strategies for the
2014-'15 MBA Application for
UC-BERKELEY HAAS

"Fill your paper with the breathings of your heart."

William Wordsworth

Did You Know?

Here are a few lesser-known factoids about UC-Berkeley's graduate business school to start things out.

- Berkeley puts an emphasis on quantitative ability in their review of an applicant. This needs to come through in many facets of your application. We discuss this throughout this *Guide*.

- Berkeley also cares a lot about culture and "school fit." To be successful in the application process, you need to understand their Defining Principles and be able to articulate how you have demonstrated them in your life. You'll hear more about that in the pages within.

- Berkeley is the only school we know of that runs contests for applicants. These often appear on Facebook. Recent ones have been "What's Your Defining Principles?" and in early summer this year they started running trivia questions every Friday. In the past, prizes have included a phone call with Admissions Director Stephanie Fujii about your application (!). Their Facebook page is haasmbaadmissions.

- Berkeley generally takes longer to review applications and render decisions within each round. This is certainly good for the applicant, as it means that they are giving each application careful consideration. It's not so good in that the decision cycle doesn't match up to other schools. A prudent Brave Supplicant should apply to other schools' subsequent rounds, even after submitting in one of the earlier Berkeley rounds, simply because you may not have your answer back from Berkeley until those other schools' deadlines will have passed.

- International applicants often have to take the TOEFL test at Berkeley, even if they would not be required to do so at other schools; this is explained on page 9. Also, a three-year undergrad from an Indian university may not be deemed sufficient by the Berkeley adcom unless you also have a Master's degree. You can still submit an application with only the three-year college experience however you may get rejected on that basis alone, given how competitive things are at this school.

- About 60% of your courses at Haas will be electives. You can choose an Area of Emphasis to study if you like, but it's not required. Haas is a general management program and you have a lot of flexibility in terms of what you choose to focus on beyond the core.

- A majority of Haas graduates stay on the West Coast. This has given the school a (slightly negative) reputation as a regional program. The school insists that the real reason for this concentration is that their students come to the Bay Area for school and they fall in love with the place; they don't want to leave when they graduate. (Have you never been to San Francisco?)

  Another truth is that if most graduates are concentrated in one area, future job opportunities will be more concentrated, too. Employers from other geographies will be less likely to recruit on campus if historical data shows that few graduates take jobs elsewhere; and, alumni who refer opportunities into the school are likely to be coming from just a few regions. The Haas brand name is not as strong overseas in Europe and Asia – nor is it even that strong on the East Coast of the U.S. This fact should be considered in your bschool selection strategy. Where do you want your career to take you? Different schools offer different opportunities across all dimensions – career focus, industry, and yes, geography.

- If you are a citizen or permanent resident, you will qualify as a California resident after your first year at Haas; so, if you make California your official home, you will qualify for reduced in-state tuition for your final year at Berkeley (it's only about $2,500, but hey! Every little bit counts.)

- Remarkably, UC-Berkeley indicated on its website in April that the tuition costs for the incoming class (the Class of 2015, starting Fall 2013) are not rising from last year's levels. Wow. There is no other school in the known universe that has not raised tuition every single year that EssaySnark has been watching things. It's a little unlikely that that will happen again next year, when you're starting your MBA, but it would be pretty great if Berkeley were able to start a trend among other schools on this.

And finally: Berkeley is the third most selective business school in the world – more selective than Wharton! The remaining pages of this *SnarkStrategies Guide* will offer you many more useful tidbits and actionable insights to give you an advantage in developing the best application possible to this unique school.

Table of Contents

Your Application to UC-Berkeley Haas 1

What You Won't Get Here 2

Know Your Target; Know Yourself 3

What Else Do You Need to Know About a
Berkeley Haas Application? 5

What Is Haas Known for? 11

Good (and Bad) Strategies for Haas 11

Which Program, Full-time or EWMBA? 18

When Should You Apply? 19

Reapplying to Haas 20

Your Berkeley Essay Strategy 21
    Step 1: Start with the career goals 21

Essay 3: Career Goals and Why Haas 32
    How to structure Haas Essay 3 37

Your Two Supporting Essays 41
    How to think about these essays 44
    Personal or professional content? 45

Essay 1: Your Transformation 48
    Should you use a failure story for essay 1? 49

Essay 2: Most Significant Professional Accomplishment 50
    Before you get too far with essays 1 and 2 51

Interviewing 52

What to Do Next 53

Your Application to UC-Berkeley Haas

Berkeley has a lot going for it, though many people underestimate exactly how hard it is to get in. Because Cal is part of the University of California system, and thus a "state school" which is generally seen as not as good as a private institution, then sometimes people misunderstand. We often encounter Brave Supplicants who consider Haas a "safety school" when compiling their list of target MBA programs. Berkeley is by no means a safety school.

Au contraire, Brave Supplicant. UC Berkeley admissions are surprisingly selective. The surprising part is not the fact that they're selective, since it's a very good school and they're looking for the just-right candidates who will fit into and contribute to their culture. What's surprising is *how* selective it is – particularly since Berkeley is often pretty far down the list of standard school rankings. EssaySnark considers Berkeley Haas to be a solidly top 10 school – we put them at #5 on our list (see http://essaysnark.com/2014/05/a-ranking-of-the-best-mba-business-schools-just-like-businessweek-does/) Not everyone would agree with this, but probably everyone would put them in the Top 15. They're most definitely not top three, yet their acceptance rate has them rubbing shoulders with the likes of Harvard and Stanford and Wharton.

With your Haas application, you need to do what you need to do with many bschool apps: You need to explain why you want an MBA, in the context of what you want to do with the degree when you graduate. You need details here. And you need to express your appreciation for and understanding of what Haas is all about. So your challenges in a Haas application are manifold.

- In some ways, Berkeley is like Stanford, which has a special way of doing things and a unique value proposition when compared to other schools.

- And in some ways, Berkeley is like Columbia, where they really want to see a plan for what you want to do with the education. You need to cover all of these elements in your essays.

If you want to go to Berkeley, you'll need to make it a priority to do significant research and learn about who they are and what they offer, and devote even more time to those essays than you probably expect. You'll need to articulate that you understand what they're about, and that you appreciate the culture, and demonstrate how you'll fit in and make a contribution.

Our opinion is that the 2014 Haas essay questions are some of the best around. That doesn't mean they will be easy! Be prepared to do a lot of writing – and a lot of *thinking* – if you're going to apply to this school.

What You Won't Get Here

This *SnarkStrategies Guide* will cover a variety of angles about Berkeley-Haas, including a discussion of those tricky essay questions, and some standard advice about visiting the program. If you've read the other *SnarkStrategies Guides* then you already know that we won't tell you what a school like this is about. You need to find that out for yourself. More directly, we will not explain or expand upon the very important Haas Defining Principles. We won't do your thinking for you; you need to apply your own thought process to the essays.

We'll tell you a story:

We had a client several years ago who, as we started working together on his Haas application, was completely misunderstanding the Defining Principles. Now, to be fair, it's easy to misunderstand them; they're a little obtuse. It often takes some wrassling to get your head around what they're about.

This client wanted to use a particular accomplishment from his professional life in his main essay. That made sense to us, and it was a fine accomplishment to be presenting to the school (he was a high-powered consultant with some high-powered story of saving an important project from a prolonged and belabored death). But, he was convinced that he was talking about one of the Defining Principles through his use of this story, and he just wasn't.

We went back and forth on it for weeks. Each time, we told him that we did not think his story fit the Defining Principle as we understood it. He was very stubborn and was insisting on doing it his way. At a certain point EssaySnark gave in. "Fine," we said. "These are your essays. You should absolutely go with what you feel is the right direction."

Hint: If you ever get that sort of feedback from us, that means you are being an idiot and we are giving up on you.

Then he attended an information session at the school. He heard some students or the admissions people or whomever talking about the Defining Principles. And he realized he was waaaaay off with how he'd been interpreting them.

It is not our job to think for you. If we work with you one-on-one as a client, we will respond to what you write and tell you if we think you've nailed it (or not). But we will never spell out to a client what they should say in an essay nor even how they should interpret the question. So we won't be doing that here either. It's up to you to interpret and reflect on the questions, and on the Defining Principles, and see where you take it in terms of your own understanding. You need to figure out where Haas is coming from on these.

There are lots of resources available from Haas about this and other aspects of their culture and their values. (Hint: Here's one: http://youtu.be/BKwjc4-CoZI) Having us regurgitate our own interpretation is not going to add value to your process. Despite the image we selected for use on this cover, it's not going to help you to parrot back what EssaySnark or anyone else has said about Haas. You need to discover it for yourself. That way, when you talk about it, your understanding will shine through and that will resonate with your audience.

So that's where we stand on that. There's still plenty of valuable information for you here.

Know Your Target; Know Yourself

Applying to bschool is not a battle (or is it?), yet still, the words of Sun Tzu apply so aptly to this situation:

> "If you know the enemy and know yourself, you need not fear the result of a hundred battles. If you know yourself but not the enemy, for every victory gained you will also suffer a defeat. If you know neither the enemy nor yourself, you will succumb in every battle."

If applying to any of the Top 20 bschools in the world, you would benefit from *visiting the school* and understanding what they're about. But there are a handful of schools in the Top 20 where it's practically mandatory that you go visit before applying. Berkeley is among them. (The others are Stanford GSB and Tuck.)

Why is this? Well for starters, let's take Berkeley's so-called *Defining Principles*.

A Snarky Caveat

> **Berkeley is different. The fact that they called them their "Defining Principles" instead of "Core Values" like everyone else does, should tell you a lot.**

Berkeley went through a rebranding campaign in 2010 that reveals a lot about the school. They are working hard to articulate how they are different from their peers, through their expression of the four "Defining Principles" which of course are integrated into their essay questions and all aspects of recruiting. Berkeley is trying to show you how they are unique. And your job, through all aspects of your application, is to show them how you are also unique.

Now, Berkeley doesn't want you to be different just for the sake of being different. You should not toss out some wacky career goals or provocative statement in your essays just so that you stand out. However, they are intentionally branding themselves around these cultural attributes which they've clearly put a lot of thought into. The Defining Principles are meant to highlight for all constituents the elements of the culture that already existed at the Haas School of Business. This is more a communications effort than a shift in who they are. It is seems significant that none of these Defining Principles has ever been articulated in connection with any other school. Haas is making a statement here.

We told you that we weren't going to do your thinking for you, but we may as well share with you a video that can help you understand where Haas is coming from. This is an admissions presentation to high school students; remember, Haas has an undergraduate program at UC-Berkeley, too. This link takes you directly to the point in this rather long presentation where this undergraduate admissions person talks about this:

http://youtu.be/ZnyiHrMpWCw?t=8m4s

See? EssaySnark is here to help. ☺

You will benefit from spending time on these Defining Principles, reflecting on them, and examining what you discover. (Quick: Can you even name them, right here and now, without peeking at the Haas website? You need to *know* them if you're applying to this school.) Consider this your official invitation to explore these values, to see what they mean to you. This is your first step in the process of articulating for yourself – and the adcom – how you are a fit to the Berkeley culture.

Another reason you should really consider visiting? Because the admissions team wants you to.

All the schools give plenty of opportunities to visit, and encourage applicants to do so – but Haas *really* encourages you. They used to have an essay question, way back in like 2008, that asked "What have you done to get to know us?" and even though they don't ask it directly very often now, they still tacitly evaluate all applications with that question in mind. Making mention of an experience you had or an insight you gained from an on-campus interaction can go far in helping the adcom see your motivation and enthusiasm. They won't penalize you if you don't visit, and it's not like you're going to get in just because you visited, but it certainly can add tremendous value on both sides of the relationship.

What Else Do You Need to Know About a Berkeley Haas Application?

Straightforward Essays

UC-Berkeley's admissions essays used to be among the most challenging of any business school anywhere – until last year, and even more so, the new ones they've released for 2014. We love the 2014 Haas application so much that we're calling them Goldilocks Essays. They're applicant-friendly in how they're phrased, yet still very challenging. It won't be trivial to come up with good answers – but you will be able to share significant parts of who you are with the adcom. And there's not too many essays to write. Last year, Haas had more essays than almost any school. This year it's the perfect number.

So many schools seem hell-bent on making their questions totally crazy ridiculously hard. Not Haas. This reveals so much of their culture.

You will even be able to get some greater bang for your buck if you do the Berkeley app first. The career goals essay you write for Berkeley will work with some minor modifications for other schools too – you still need to do a lot of tweaking and massaging but the messaging in your pitch should translate quite well. This would include Columbia, UCLA, and Tuck, and potentially even Stanford. Again, no word-for-word re-use is ever possible, but adaption of what you have to say about your future intentions certainly is.

What remains true about Haas – and just a warning, this is the main place people trip up – is that you need to know what the school is about before you write one word of an essay draft. This can make the adcom's job easy, when someone does a sloppy job on the essays. They can instantly tell that the person is not a good fit for the school. Your biggest challenge then is in figuring out exactly what Berkeley means by their four Defining Principles – and identifying relevant stories from your own past to use to express that understanding.

We go into detail on the Haas essay questions in this *SnarkStrategies Guide* however we won't define the Defining Principles for you. It's up to you to dig into them and reflect on them and *relate to them* through your treatment of your profile in your essays.

Focus on GMAT and Especially Quant

They also have a marked focus on GMAT scores, particularly quant scores, and quant skills overall. They are signaling this clearly with the questions the ask on the application about quant classes and experience. This amount of emphasis is unusual.

We don't think Haas actually cares about quant skills more than any other great school. All the schools want to ensure that their students have the foundational quant skills needed to succeed in their curriculum. Haas is simply more outward and direct about indicating this than other schools are. They even have an Optional Essay specifically asking for applicants to detail their previous quantitative experiences. (They experimented with removing this question from the application one year but have since restored it; yes, it's that important.)

Haas cares about the quant. And the verbal. And the AWA and the IR. The whole enchilada, frankly.

So, what's a good GMAT score for UC-Berkeley?

The average GMAT score is 714 for the Class of 2015 (the last data available at the time of this writing); it's been in the 715-718 range since the 2008 application season. This average is nearly as high as the best programs; by comparison, MIT's average GMAT was 713 for Class of 2015; Yale is now up to 719; Harvard, Stanford, and Wharton are higher. The 80% range at Haas is generally 680 to 760, which is a tighter band than many comparable schools. If you're below a 680 total, it may be tough to get an offer at this school. They have a small class and so it's harder for them to absorb too many students with very low GMAT scores. You can expect only a handful to be accepted every year.

To offer more granularity:

- A quant score of at least 46 is recommended as a bare-minimum. A couple years ago, we heard Haas admissions state that they wanted to see a 45 – however that was many years ago, and things are more competitive. Today, a 45Q is only at the 63rd percentile, which, sorry guys, is just not that impressive. When Haas gave that recommendation, a 45Q was 68th percentile. Yes, things have heated up that much in just a few short years.

- A verbal score of at least 35 is recommended. The verbal is also important but not quite as critical. If you're an international applicant, then you almost definitely will need to take the TOEFL for this school, which will give them another measure of your language skills. An international student can expect that the GMAT verbal will be examined in conjunction with the TOEFL to make sure that everything is being reinforced as they would expect. If your GMAT verbal and/or TOEFL scores are too low, then the adcoms may wonder if the essays come in too perfect. Be careful about using the services of any admissions consultant or essay agency that is too heavy-handed in their editing.

The Haas admissions committee asks a variety of supplemental questions, some of which seem like mini-essays of their own.

The most important is the second Optional Essay asking about quant skills. This is an opportunity for you. If it's not obvious that you've got the analytical chops to succeed in bschool based on your undergrad studies, GMAT, career history, or a combination of all that, then you really should take advantage of that essay. If your skills are being communicated very vividly through those application assets, then don't bother. Many people will want to include the second Optional Essay, however.

If you're in either of these situations then we recommend definitely writing that essay:

a) **Your quant score is 45 or below.** If you have a decent GMAT score but it's entirely made up of a strong showing on the verbal side, you MUST submit an answer to this essay question.

b) **If your quant score is 47 or below** and you've never done any quantitative or heavily analytical work in your career, you might also consider answering this question.

c) **If you failed any quant class in college** (statistics, calculus, economics, etc.), or even if you got a very poor grade in such a class, you might want to answer this question. You should also consider taking a quant-based class now, before you apply, to shore up your skills and reinforce your profile in this area.

d) **If you are in your 30s and** have been out of school for ten years or so and have little evidence of quant skills obvious in your profile, again you might consider answering this question for the adcom.

Note that if you're able to fit in this information about your quant skills in the main essays (or if you're confident that your recommenders have covered this for you in their letters of recommendation), you need not do this optional question – but it never hurts. Most people should go ahead and volunteer this information.

Snarky Strategy #1

If you never took calc or stats, and you don't use numbers on the job in any meaningful way, then you should strongly consider taking a quant-based class before applying to Berkeley.

If you knocked the GMAT out of the park, then no, you probably don't need to take a separate class. But if you didn't, if your background doesn't instantly show the adcom how you've worked with numbers before, it certainly couldn't hurt to buff up your profile with a class. It demonstrates your commitment to this process, and it would likely help you be that much more successful once you're starting bschool, too.

Many schools would appreciate this addition to your profile. Some schools even require admitted students to take such a class before they matriculate. Berkeley wants to see evidence of this education *when you apply*. And, it's definitely more useful to them to see a grade from a completed class, than simply a statement that the class is in progress. So plan ahead and take a class if you feel your profile needs bolstering in this area.

It doesn't matter if you take an in-person classroom-based class or an online class; they just want to see that it's a challenging course covering the appropriate material. Cal even has some self-paced courses available through Berkeley Extension (see http://extension.berkeley.edu/static/math/) that may be perfect for you. We do not recommend using a MOOC course such as through Coursera or Udacity as a way to boost your quant profile. Go for a formal course at an accredited college.

A Snarky Caveat

> Haas has a preference for very traditionally-quant classes like calculus and statistics. Accounting and finance are fine but they don't carry quite the same weight with the admissions committee.

Emphasis on Significant Work Experience

Berkeley is one of the "older" MBA programs in terms of average age of their students. Most students in the full-time program have around five years of work experience. Haas will consider an application from someone much younger, but they send strong signals in many places on their website that they prefer more work experience. If you're in your mid-20s, then you'd need to not only express how you're at the right stage of your life to benefit from the Haas MBA, but you'd also need to show how you've achieved a lot already in your life – beyond what others your age have. And, your GMAT and GPA likely will need to be higher than someone who's got a more standard work experience profile. The adcom will be looking for more from you if you apply at a younger age.

This is not to say that you shouldn't give it a shot, but you'll have your work cut out for you. If you're determined to go to bschool right now, then maybe you'll want to look into other schools that are more accommodating of younger candidates (Harvard, Chicago, and perhaps MIT are the standard choices). Of course, for "older" candidates who have five years or more, UC-Berkeley can be very welcoming.

At least three years of solid work experience is recommended before seriously considering Berkeley for your MBA.

Some Hurdles for Indian Applicants

Two areas where the standard Indian applicant will be at a disadvantage at UC-Berkeley:

- They do not accept the three-year undergraduate degree conferred by some Indian universities. Four-year degrees from India are acceptable. If all you have is an Indian undergraduate education without an additional master's, then you may not qualify for admission to UC-Berkeley. A number of other bschools will accept an application from you, but Berkeley may not find your educational background sufficient. You should review their policies as outlined in the FAQ on the website (http://mba.haas.berkeley.edu/admissions/faq.html) to see which schools and degrees may or may not be suitable.

- They have a stricter requirement on the TOEFL exam if you did not receive a degree in an English-speaking country. If all your education was in India (or China, or Pakistan, or a bunch of other places) and you have not gotten a master's degree, for example, from a country where the official language is English – the U.S., the UK, Canada, Australia, etc. – then you must take the TOEFL exam as part of your application to UC-Berkeley. This requirement holds even if you have worked in the U.S. for many years. If your education was not in a country where English is the official language, you'll need to take the test. The TOEFL is easy for anyone with strong language skills, so it's not going to be a big deal for you. You should probably take the GMAT first, since studying for the verbal section and the AWA help you prepare for the TOEFL thereafter.

Our understanding is that these requirements are set by Cal; there is no way for Haas to waive them for a candidate, so don't even ask.

Relatively Small Applicant Pool

The good news is that Berkeley doesn't get a huge number of applications each year. Recently it's been in the 3,400 apps range. Apps went up nearly 4% last year, to about 3,500. This is still an impressive number – by comparison, Yale gets only around 2,700 or 2,800 and they're filling a larger class – however the Berkeley volumes are half as many as Stanford. The Haas admissions team has reported that the quality of the applicant pool has been increasing in recent years.

Still, because of the smaller overall volume of applications, it's relatively easy for a strong candidate to stand out. If you apply in their first round, you have an even better chance of being noticed, since they get the smallest number of pitches then.

Different Profiles for the Different Programs

Here are some basic stats about Haas:

- About 250 students in the full-time 21-month MBA
- About 250 students in the three-year EWMBA part-time program for employed individuals
- About 70 students in the Berkeley MBA for Executives

If you're already in the Bay Area and you're committed to going to Haas – and your profile is a little weak in either the GPA or GMAT area – and, you're up for the intensity that getting your MBA while working involves – then you might consider trying for their EWMBA (Evenings & Weekend) part-time MBA. There is less competition for this program and a strong candidate should have a relatively "easy" time getting an offer ("easy" is in quotes because it's never easy to get into any top MBA program). Haas does not let you switch between tracks; if you get into EWMBA, you get the same education, but you have to complete the entire MBA curriculum under the EWMBA program.

This *SnarkStrategies Guide* focuses on admissions to the full-time and part-time MBA tracks, since profiles of successful applicants tend to be somewhat similar between the two. There are also some significant differences, which are covered later in this *Guide*.

The Berkeley Executive MBA is also relatively easier to gain admission to. A full discussion of the EMBA track is outside the scope of this *SnarkStrategies Guide*, however if you have a question about it, feel free to send an email to gethelpnow@essaysnark.com or post on the EssaySnark blahg at http://essaysnark.com.

What Is Haas Known for?

Berkeley-Haas has particular strength in the innovative fields of:

- Technology – as you would expect, given the close proximity to Silicon Valley
- Entrepreneurship – not just tech ventures, but other types as well
- Social Ventures – given UC-Berkeley's deep history of social activism
- Cleantech – the burgeoning field of alternative energy and all things "green"
- Healthcare – with a well-respected joint Masters of Public Health also available

Above all, Berkeley is a general management program, and you can do a multitude of things coming out with a Haas MBA. We'll let you discover the details about each of these areas through your own research, but they're the broad categories that Haas has a special expertise in.

Good (and Bad) Strategies for Haas

Let's start with some common bschool application strategies that apply at Haas – and some that won't fly. The first is less a strategy, and more an invitation (encouragement? admonition?) to be genuine.

Be Authentically Enthusiastic

(Try saying that five times fast.)

This is smart advice at any school – so much so, that it really shouldn't be considered a "strategy." It should be in the category of *just be you.* By that we mean, figure out who you are, and figure out why you want to go to the school, and let that shine through your application. (Easier said than done, we realize.)

Showing honest conviction and excitement for any school is important, but it's really really important at Haas. Here's why:

> While Haas has a very low acceptance rate, they also have a relatively low yield.

Yield is the percentage of applicants that a school accepts, that also accepts them. In other words, it's the percentage of accepted applicants who say "yes" and enroll. A few schools like Harvard have ridiculously high yields in the 89% range; pretty much anyone accepted to

Harvard is going to go to Harvard. The further you move down the list of bschool rankings, the lower the yield tends to go – and, the proportionally more applicants a school must accept in order to guarantee that they'll fill their class.

Haas' yield is less than 60%, which means they have to accept about 50% more applicants than their target class size, as a "buffer" in order to get their desired 240 students each year.

What does this mean for you as an applicant? One direct implication of Haas' relatively low yield is that they carefully examine applications to see if there is true commitment from the candidate and intent to actually accept an offer should they extend one.

If you make sloppy mistakes, such as re-using another school's essay and neglecting to change the other school's name ("I really want to go to Yale because..."), it's going to be difficult for Haas to accept you. Or, if they cannot see evidence that you have done your homework and put forth some effort to learn about them – if you cannot appropriately articulate their Defining Principles, say – they're going to be hard pressed to make an offer.

The best way to demonstrate this type of enthusiasm? Doing your research on the school, understanding what they're about, and engaging in some self-reflection so that you communicate what YOU'RE about.

To figure out how to do all THAT... just keep reading.

Misguided Application Strategies

Here are some common application strategies we see for Haas candidates – and some gotchas associated with each:

1. **Applying to Berkeley and Stanford in a bid to stay in the Bay Area.** Unfortunately both these programs have seriously competitive admissions, so it's quite common for a candidate to come up short if there's only these two schools on their list. Be prepared for a lot of work – and possible disappointment – if you're targeting just these two.

2. **Applying to Berkeley along with Harvard and Wharton and treating Haas as a "safety school." We covered this already.** This is a misunderstanding of reality. Haas is never a "safety school." It is often harder to get into Haas than Wharton!

3. **Applying to Berkeley to do finance** – and talking too much about New York in your essays. Sure, some Haas graduates end up on Wall Street. But not many. If you are targeting a finance career, and you're not planning to stay in the Bay Area when you graduate, you might want to mention what your plans are and what resources you'll leverage to find your plum NYC gig. And, recognize that the adcom will assume you're also applying to Columbia and NYU if you talk about NYC *too* much;

they'll think you're re-using an essay for one of those schools for your Haas application. You could still succeed in a bid for Haas but you'll have to show them the love and convince them that they are your first choice school (you cannot merely state this, you need to demonstrate it through how you present yourself on paper). Finally, you may want to read this post on the EssaySnark blahg about an obvious but often overlooked contradiction for a wanna-be Wall Streeter to be ushing and gushing about the Haas culture:

http://essaysnark.com/2014/03/culture-columbia-nyc-and-wall-street/

4. **Applying to Berkeley to do cleantech.** Haas is one of the first schools to offer support to those interested in renewable and alternative energy, and they also have a very strong technology and engineering (and entrepreneurship) focus. However, if you want to go into cleantech, you must recognize that there just aren't that many jobs available. It's a new industry. It's hard to break into – even with the advantage of a Haas MBA. As a starting point, you need to have a relevant background that shows you can make the leap into this exciting field based on your own transferable skills and experience. And, you need to realize that there are limited jobs available, and a lot of high-energy (pardon the pun!) motivated bschool candidates claiming to want to go into this area. You'll need to impress the Haas adcom on multiple levels if you're targeting cleantech as your post-MBA career.

5. **Applying to Berkeley without visiting.** As we said earlier, you don't *need* to fly out to California in order to be admitted, but it's the very best way to understand what this school is about. Just like with Stanford, UC-Berkeley has a specific culture that they are clearly working to emphasize through the focus on their Defining Principles in the essay questions. This is best understood by going through an info session on campus. Or, you could attend one if the school travels to a city near you; it's not mandatory that you literally set foot in California to benefit. You should make a point to attend one somewhere though. The school does a lot with online chats and helpful information on the website, but none of these are a direct substitute for actually hearing the students or admissions team speak about the school themselves.

If you were thinking of heading down any of those roads, make sure you assess your strategy carefully, so that you're not left all dressed up and nowhere to go at the end of the application season.

Efficient Multi-School Strategies

Snarky Strategy #2

If you're also applying to UCLA or Columbia – do that application first.

Even though you will be writing essays from scratch when applying to multiple schools (you will be doing that, right?), you might find it efficient to adapt the Anderson or Columbia or maybe NYU career goals essays (or potentially Ross's; we haven't seen the 2014 questions yet but last year theirs was good for this). You could do these the other way around – complete Haas first and then adapt it to another school – however there's some reasons for getting one of the others out of the way first:

- One: Your first application is likely to be the toughest. It takes awhile to get the knack of writing your bschool essays. However, your essay-writing skills will improve as you get through the first application. The work you do on the first school will pay off as you tackle the next. Since Haas is so darn competitive, you might not want to tackle them as your first project. You need every advantage that you can get with Haas.

- Two: Because the Haas career goals question goes into some unique territory, it might be easier to do another more "basic" version of the question and then move over to see how you'll need to modify it for Berkeley.

These are just suggestions. The work you do on your Haas application will also help you craft stronger essays for other schools too, so it's fine if you begin with this one.

What's Important at Haas

Since you've already started to do your research, you should be able to easily identify the following elements and qualities as very important at this school.

- Leadership
- Innovation
- Ethics
- Humility
- Emotional Intelligence

These traits are evident through the language they use on their website, through their Defining Principles, and through their tagline of "Leading Through Innovation."

You don't necessarily have to emphasize each one of these traits separately in your application, however you should have an awareness of these qualities, and you need to articulate why they are important to you in your choice of Haas. These are all somewhat slippery concepts, too. You might want to take a moment now and see if you can define for yourself what each of them mean.

- For example, we caught a tweet from Dean Lyons a few years back that said: "Leader: someone who makes the people around her better." This is just one of many facets to the idea of *leadership*.

- Another hint: The principle of "Students Always" is not about staying in school for the rest of your life. If you talk about this Defining Principle in your essays, don't just tell the adcom that you're currently taking a class. It's a *mindset*.

In the aftermath of accusations levied against the bschools that they contributed to the 2008 economic crisis, Dean Lyons is particularly sensitive to ethics and attitude. The Haas adcom is going to be screening everything you say in your application through that filter. This is one reason why they have students and alumni do the interviewing for the full-time program; they want to be sure that the candidate fits in with the student culture. This is best evaluated by students themselves.

Haas is also about *leadership* and they are perhaps more upfront about it than many schools. Sure, leadership is a big deal at all top schools, but not all the schools put quite so much focus on it in their outreach materials and how they present their value proposition. You'll need to have examples of how you've demonstrated leadership qualities already in your life, in order to make a convincing pitch at Haas.

Given their location, you would expect some of the trends and the overall zeitgeist of Silicon Valley would permeate the culture at Haas, and it certainly has. After all, there's high interest in entrepreneurship at this school, and rock star entrepreneur Steve Blank began his teaching career at Berkeley (or maybe it was Stanford? Ah, irrelevant!) We recently heard a Haas admissions person speaking in the language common to the startup community these days which is so focused on "failing fast." She said they are "looking for students who aren't afraid of risk and also not afraid to fail. We want people who question the status quo on a daily basis."

If you can show yourself as one of those people, you will be ahead of the pack in the race for an admit from Haas.

Another buzzword that Haas has adopted lately? "Path-bending." Here's the prompt for the essay that you'll get to write for scholarship consideration once you're admitted to the program:

> *Our mission at Berkeley-Haas is to develop innovative leaders who redefine how we do business. What makes you, as Dean Rich Lyons says, "a path-bending leader"? Please demonstrate your strong potential for business, economic, or governmental leadership in your home country. How will Haas serve as a catalyst for that potential compared to other schools to which you have been admitted?*

We do not think that you should use the phrase "path-bending" anywhere in your essays – it's debatable whether that phrase should even appear in the scholarship essay. This is because it just sounds so darned cocky.

However, an understanding of what that's pointing to can only help you as you analyze your raw material and see what might qualify for coverage as a Berkeley-Haas essay topic.

The Best Advice We Can Offer for a Successful Berkeley App

We've already told you that UC-Berkeley wants you to know what they're about before you apply. They really like it when candidates come visit ahead of submitting an application. They do recognize that this is not always possible, and they do not penalize you if you're unable to do so. However, they emphasize a campus visit so much in their website that it indicates how valuable they feel it is.

If you cannot visit campus ahead of time, you must-must-must find other ways to learn about the school and interact with students. UC-Berkeley has a variety of channels available for this, from online chats and podcasts and short video FAQs from students about the culture and community, to their Student Ambassador program where you can ask a current student a question via email, to YouTube videos like this one http://youtu.be/pAkUKletxGs (warning, that video is loooooong and a bit boring – don't worry, Haas is not boring! They just have a PR department that became enamored of converting pictures to video with nifty transitions and a soundtrack). You should also reach out to any Haas alumni that you know, to find out more about this program and what their experience was like.

All your efforts to learn about the school will pay off as a greater understanding of how a Haas education is different and what this school is about in terms of its mission in the world.

A Snarky Caveat

If you're going to participate in an online chat and you signed up with your real name, be sure you don't say something stupid.

We are big fans of honesty in living life, but as you know, we also operate on the Internet under a pseudonym. You might want to do that, too, if you're signing in for an online chat with Haas or any other school. Sometimes people say dumb things on a chat – and yes those admissions people pay attention. If you are signed on as you – Mortimer Foxundhound II – then we're guessing that the admissions people will remember that name (and the lame-o question you asked) when your MBA application hits their desk. Sometimes people ask outright idiotic questions, and sometimes they just phrase their question in a way that makes them sound immature. Remember that EQ (emotional intelligence) is a key part of a successful application to any good school these days, and this is especially true at Haas.

Here's an example of what someone asked in a recent Berkeley chat: "I've worked for 5 years now, and have some very good experience down on my resume. With this impressive resume, how much will it matter if my academic record isn't great?"

Innocent question, right? And probably not a deal-killer if the adcom connected this comment with this person's application later. But this person does sound a little cocky, no? Maybe just a tiny bit? Perhaps a little sense of entitlement showing?

This is a small point, perhaps on the trivial side. We do encourage you to participate in those chats. And sure, you can do so under your real name – but please be careful. There are very few new and novel questions that are ever asked in a chat, so it's not like you're going to sacrifice being remembered for how smart you are or what an insightful question you posed to them. That seems like the only possible advantage in using your real name, and it's a slim one indeed. Instead, you may want to play it safe. Don't sign onto an online chat (or online discussion board, or blog, or anything else for that matter) under your true name. It's the smallest thing that could prevent a bigger hiccup in your quest for bschool.

And remember: You can be Googled at any time. Hopefully your Facebook page is not too incriminating these days...

Which Program, Full-time or EWMBA?

Back to weightier subjects.

Berkeley has several MBA options to choose from. Whether you go for a full-time MBA or a part-time program has as much to do with your career goals and your personal circumstances as it does the acceptance rate of the target program. Usually (but not always) full-time programs are better for career-changers, since they offer the internship opportunity that can give you important experience in your new field. Usually (but not always) it's more common for those who are sponsored by their current employers to choose a part-time program, since they can keep working while simultaneously earning their MBA. We've heard of people do internships during Haas EWMBA and there are always sponsored students in F/T, so these are not rules by any means.

If you're trying to figure out which Haas program *you have a better chance at*, then there are many factors to consider. Admissions policies at the different MBA tracks at UC-Berkeley are similar, but different. The applications are different, the deadlines and processes are different, and they are managed by different admissions teams. The profile of student that each is looking for is somewhat different, too.

Besides the fact that EWMBA students are usually local, and are all working full-time while pursuing their MBA studies, the main difference from full-time is that EWMBA students tend to be quite a bit older, with the average age around 32. This means that they have about eight years of work experience. Students in the full-time program typically have five years of experience, and the average age is 28. This has held steady for many years now. It's unlikely that Berkeley will start accepting candidates who are significantly younger for either of these tracks (note that the EWMBA track does have a wide range of student, generally from 25 through 44 years of age).

Additional differences between these programs?

- There is less scholarship money available to the part-time EWMBA folks since they're working; the common wisdom is that they have more resources available to pay for the education, especially since many are getting help from their employers to go through the program (about 66% have some form of financial sponsorship from their job). Note, though, that reduced in-state tuition for California residents is *not* available for EWMBA students based on how the program is classified by the University.

- Also due to University rules, EWMBA students are also not allowed to take classes outside of the bschool. And, for the most part, the EWMBA curriculum is separate from the full-time track. EWMBA students can take certain electives with F/T students however based purely on scheduling constraints – the "evenings and weekends" part – part-timers are mostly with their own through the course of the program.

- On-campus recruiting is open to EWMBA students (this is not true at all top bschools that have part-time programs). An internship is even possible as an EWMBA student if you're willing to quit your current job in your final year of studies to do it.

- You need not live in the Bay Area to participate in the EWMBA program. Students fly in from as far away as Southern California, Seattle, and even Colorado. Note that this is also true of the corollary program at UCLA Anderson called the FEMBA ("Fully-Employed MBA"), and Anderson now has an even more flexible option called, appropriately enough, FEMBA Flex. These might be good to explore you're in the Western U.S. and planning on keeping your current job while pursuing your MBA; it's currently easier to get into FEMBA and it is to get into EWMBA, though a strong applicant will find it straightforward to get an offer from either or both.

You can only apply to one MBA program at Berkeley at a time. You'll need to decide which is the right one for you and commit to it. You cannot switch between the part-time and the full-time programs or vice versa (you used to be able to do this but they changed the rules recently). And, if you don't make it into one and decide to try for the other at a later time, you'll need to offer a good reason for your change in strategy (see section below on Reapplying to Haas).

When Should You Apply?

Berkeley is unique in having four rounds for the full-time program. This gives you a bit more flexibility in terms of your overall application strategy. The aspect that is not in your favor is that each Haas round extends later than most schools; they take longer to issue decisions than many other schools do.

To wit: The Haas first-round decisions may not officially be rendered until as late as mid-January. They often issue acceptance decisions earlier than this but they don't guarantee that they will do so. This compares to many other first-round decisions from most other schools coming a full month earlier, in mid-December. This means that if you apply in Round 1 at Haas, you would be wise to also plan for a Round 2 application at another school, just as a risk mitigation strategy. You are not likely to get your Haas decision until *after* those other apps are due. Even interview invitations might come very late in the cycle, so you could be left in the dark about how the Haas app will turn out for longer than you'd like.

In terms of getting a round advantage at Berkeley, as with other schools, you should apply in Round 1 (October) or Round 2 (January). Round 3 is basically too late to have a real shot of admission; there won't be many slots left at that point, and only the most very impressive candidate will have a chance. Plus, you'll have little opportunity for financial help. International students especially MUST apply in Rounds 1 or 2 if they want a real chance.

The admissions office has stated publicly that applying in the last round is a disadvantage since they have mostly filled the class by then. This is primarily true for the standard full-time program; sometimes there are more spots open in the last round for EWMBA admissions. A very strong domestic candidate might be OK in Round 3 but it's much much riskier. If your GMAT or GPA is low, avoid applying in that final cycle, and instead consider waiting it out for the first round in the next season.

Reapplying to Haas

If you applied unsuccessfully to one of the Berkeley MBA programs within the last two years, you are considered a reapplicant if you try again at any of their programs. You'll need to investigate the reapplicant policy for the program you're interested in targeting now (either EWMBA or full-time). They do not typically require it, but they will accept a full set of new essays from you if you are motivated to tackle them all anew.

Very important: If you're switching to try your luck in admissions at the other program from where you originally applied – in other words, if you didn't make it into the full-time MBA and now you want to go for the EWMBA – you'll need to articulate a valid reason why now the other program is the right fit for you. This can trip people up sometimes. Be sure you're able to explain why now this other program makes sense for where you're at in your career and with your career goals.

Same thing with career goals at Haas: If you radically change what you're planning to do post-MBA in your reapplicant essay, then you need to explain how you came up with this new plan. The Haas adcom will absolutely look at your original application and compare it with your new one. You need to explain the deltas.

Because Haas typically changes its essays each year, it is a good idea for reapplicants submit all new essays. You definitely need to update them on changes and progress, to show how you've improved your profile since the first time; use one of their several optional essays for that. Haas is open to reapplicants and will look carefully at your candidacy to see if you might make the cut this time, so you should go for it if Haas is still on your short list of target schools. A full reapplicant strategy is out of scope here however we have a separate book to help you: *The Reapplicant's Guide* is available in the EssaySnark Bookstore.

Your Berkeley Essay Strategy

This is supposed to be a guide to the Berkeley essays, so let's get on with those essays, shall we?

Step 1: Start with the career goals

Even though the career goals is the last Haas essay question, it is definitely not the least important. You can see that based on how much they are asking you to say. The detailed sub-parts to the prompt are going to be so helpful in guiding you to developing a good, useful set of answers to this question. The only gripe we would have about the Haas career goals essay this year is that they've cut it short, while also adding to the complexity with the three sub-parts. Since this year's version of career goals is focused exclusively on your immediate post-MBA job, then you're going to be OK; you're not to talk about long-term goals in the Haas essay at all (well OK, you could do so, but it's not mandatory, and it's certainly not what they have asked for).

Here's the question:

> *What is your desired post-MBA role and at what company or organization?*
>
> *a. How is your background compelling to this company?*
>
> *b. What is something you would do better for this company than any other employee?*
>
> *c. Why is an MBA necessary and how will Haas specifically help you succeed at this company?* (500-600 words inclusive)

Last year Haas gave people 750 words for goals, short- and long-term both – which, admittedly, was probably more than necessary. This year though, you may find yourself strapped to cover everything that they're asking for in those sub-questions within just the 500 to 600 words they're offering. Most people will need to use the full 600 words. If you come up much lighter than that, then we're going to suggest that you probably didn't answer each question sufficiently.

Even though 600 words may still not feel like much when you're writing them, in this era of short essays, you will find this length to be a real luxury. We appreciate how difficult it is for the adcom to go through applications, and thus their desire to keep things short. Shorter essays may also seem more enticing to an applicant who hasn't started to actually write them yet. However, it's not necessarily helping BSers when the essay requirements are so slim. We are pleased to see a few schools holding out with these more permissive lengths.

What is the most important part of this three-part question?

While parts a and b are important, if only because the school has asked about them, we're going to go out on a limb with a brazen claim that part c of Haas Essay 3 is the most important. Why? Because it lets you talk about Haas. This is pretty much the only place you'll get to do so in the essays. You could mention Haas-specific stuff in the others but space is pretty limited there and you'll likely need to dedicate yourself to simply answering those questions without the luxury of including any nice-to-have content in those.

Berkeley wants you to go beyond the basics. With the entirety of this Essay 3 question, they want you to provide examples from your existing career around how and why you're ready for the transition to the MBA and beyond. The reason that part a isn't therefore the "most important" part of Essay 3 is because you will get to communicate some of this awesomeness quite easily in Essay 2. That essay is going to carry a lot of your application weight for you. Thus, the background info is being conveyed in multiple places, so what you say in response to part a is not quite as mission-critical as it would otherwise be. (If there were no "significant accomplishments" question in the other essays of the set, then we would've said that part a is the most important of Essay 3.)

Beyond learning about you, the Haas adcom also wants to see evidence of what you've done to learn about their program and why you're convinced it's the right school for you. This essay is the key opportunity for you to convey this. You have a blank slate with this essay. Take advantage of it. Talk about what literally excites you about the school and their program. Go into some details. Make them happy that they've read your application because of all the enthusiasm you express for what they're about. Tell them what you learned when you visited. Tailor this essay explicitly to the Berkeley advantage and what you believe it will do for you, and you'll go far in communicating to them why you might belong at the Haas School of Business.

Sometimes people forget the whole notion that an MBA is designed for a purpose: To help you go from where you are today, to somewhere else.

Do you know where that "somewhere else" is?

And do you know how the target MBA program will enable that journey for you?

If you don't know, you'd better find out.

Because it's kinda silly, isn't it, that you'd be applying for an MBA without really knowing what for? Lots of people get stars in their eyes about wanting an MBA, but without sitting down to figure out why you need one, and why THIS SCHOOL is the place to get it, you're not going to get very far in the admissions process.

At least, not at Haas. (Not at Duke, either, BTW.)

So, when tackling your Haas essays, you should probably begin with this career goals question, even though it's the last one they ask. The reason to do this is because it's the most important essay. Your career goals serve as the backbone for your entire application strategy.

You will want to test your answers to the other questions against this one, to see if they are properly reinforcing and supporting your career goals pitch, if you already have the career goals pitched.

Snarky Strategy #3

Start your Haas essay development with the question on goals, then go back to the shorter ones.

Here's how to do that.

EssaySnark's career goals exercise for new clients

This is an exercise we ask new clients to complete. This will serve you well as you begin to craft your answer to the Haas career goals question – in fact, it will serve you in tackling the goals question that any school asks, in any form or variety.

> Please complete this fill-in-the-blank exercise. This is a good first step for you to develop your ideas for career goals, in order to demonstrate to the adcom what you want to do and why an MBA is essential:
>
> **1. "After I get my MBA I will be/do X"**
>
> Add as much detail as you can - job title, industry or niche, functional area, specialty, example companies to work for, geography, etc.
>
> *[Write your answer here. Go ahead. Nobody will look at it.]*
>
> _____
>
> _____
>
> _____
>
> _____
>
> **2. "My long term goal is to do Y"**
>
> Less detail needed, but must be clear and specific, and rational, given the s/t goal.
>
> *[Write this one down, too – even though it's not part of the question being asked.]*
>
> _____
>
> _____
>
> _____

3. "An MBA from Berkeley-Haas is critical for me to achieve this because: "

Solid reasons that point to the differentiation offered by Haas are critical here — you'll want to express how it will explicitly give you the skills you need for the short-term goal.

[This is important. Focus on the short-term goal only here. Use more space if you need to.]

_____

_____

_____

_____

4. "Now is the right time for me to get an MBA because: "

A younger candidate would include a quick statement of why they feel they're ready, other candidates might describe how they need the MBA now to take advantage of the opportunities they see in their industry; all candidates should focus on career milestones, significant professional achievements, and other signs of "readiness" to show how you're at a point in your career where you will benefit from the MBA — this can be answered in a lot of different ways, so see what you can come up with on the "why now?" side.

[This is explicit in this year's Haas career goals question – it's embedded in the "how are you compelling?" bit.]

_____

_____

_____

_____

> The short-term goal should have significant detail, and the bschool experience needs to be the setup for that (bschool should be positioned as the best means possible to prepare you for that s/t goal). The long-term goal needs much less detail but it needs to be logical and achievable, given the interim goals. You wouldn't want to position bschool as prep for the l/t goal, only the short-term one.

Funny, that third prompt... Call us crazy, but to us, doesn't it somehow tangentially in some way resemble the question that UC-Berkeley is asking you to cover in part c of Essay 3?

Weird.

Or not.

Yes, it's true, Brave Supplicant. EssaySnark has been using this exercise with clients FOR YEARS to help them identify why they want an MBA from a specific school – yet this year, 2014, with Berkeley Haas, it's the first time that any school has actually asked the question in such a similar way.

Lots of schools ask "Why us?" and in fact with Stanford, that's pretty much the only question you get from them. Those questions are asking the same thing. Seeing the Haas version, though... well that just warms the cockles of EssaySnark's little heart. (We don't know what "cockles" are. And you may be surprised to learn that we have a heart. But whatever.)

Also, we are exceedingly gratified to see that finally a school is asking for more specifics around role and organization. These are details that we've been coaching candidates to include for, like, forever. (Remember that Harvard does NOT expect to see this level of detail; their admissions director has even scoffed at the idea of having a "laminated life plan" - but all schools are different! And UC-Berkeley wants to see that you've put some thought into this! So "laminated life plan" it is!)

Specificity can take you far with Haas, and this year, it's mandatory. Going into that level of detail – like, including an actual "title" in what you say about your short-term goal – this shows that you've put some thought into this plan, that you've researched the options, that you know the industry. That level of detail is so important here.

Clearly, you should spend some time on this. What most people come up with their first time out is far from sufficient. You may even need to go off and do some research on your target industry and find out what types of jobs are available and what you'd be doing in them. Use LinkedIn. Talk to people. Do some digging. Flesh this out.

An off-the-cuff set of career goals will not help you get into Haas.

So what's a bad career goal?

Let's look at a few examples.

> "I want to become a leader in the financial services industry."

We see this all the time. Sorry folks. "Leader" is meaningless. And, believe it or not, so is "financial services." Much too broad. Are you talking about a big bank? A hedge fund? A mutual fund or other investment management company? Even insurance companies are often lumped into "financial services." This sentence is near-meaningless. It doesn't tell us anything about *what you want to do*.

Here's another one:

> "I want to be on the executive team of a multinational corporation."

Same problem. Sure, "executive team" has a little more specificity than "leader" however it still doesn't tell us *what you want to do*. (Note the theme?) And "multinational corporation" is just a blob of a term. What type of corporation? In which country? If you're interested in some type of international angle to your career, then you need to say that! This term is communicating next to nothing — except to say that maybe you haven't really put that much thought into it yet.

The other issue with both of these "bad" examples (probably) is timing. It's unrealistic to assume you'll be much of a "leader" — at least, not on a grand scale or anything — within the timeframe that Berkeley is asking you to present with these career goals. Remember, they're not asking about long-term goals at all. They want to know what you're going to do immediately.

Nobody can see the future. Nobody knows what you'll be doing in 15 years. And yet that's how long it would take for most people to gain the experience, skills, and connections to actually become a CFO or what have you. It's highly unlikely you'll be rocking that boat within the timeframe expected in a "short/long-term goals" question from any school. So, saying you'll be on the ELT of a big conglomerate is a little unrealistic, probably.

Instead, you need to focus on literally what type of job you'll get right when you come out of Haas. If you want to be uber-prepared, then you can also carve out a plan for how you'll progress from that first job, to perhaps another position, and at most, one more, which would be your long-term target. That final job that you present as your long-term goal should be within a reasonable timeframe. The foreseeable future. Like, maybe ten years from now, max (even that is not really "foreseeable" given how quickly things change in our lives and the world these days). Sometimes these questions do come up in interviews, so it doesn't hurt to map all this out now, even though you're not going to be talking about it in the actual essay. You may decide to cover this in the Haas Dean's Fellowship essay though, once you've been admitted (yes we are always the optimist!). We have a separate short strategy guide that can help you with that essay when the time comes; look for it in The Bookstore on essaysnark.com.

On your goals and the overall career progression from where you sit today: Keep in mind that most people are promoted maybe once every two years. If you consider your long-term goal to be in the five- to eight-year post-MBA timeframe, that will help you see (hopefully) what might be a realistic target to present for the adcom.

Given where you're at today in your career (level/role/title/responsibilities), what is a probable trajectory for you to end up in, say, the year 2025? What is a reasonable step-by-step track that you see your career might go through?

One exception where it might fly to tell the adcom that you'll be "CEO"? If you're going to be working in a family business after you graduate. If that's the case, then it's fine to say you're going to be taking over the whole show. You have different challenges than most people in presenting your goals (which are outside the discussion of this guide) however this could work well in being realistic and believable.

Wait – what did we just say? Something about "realistic and believable"? Yes, that sounds good. This is something to make note of formally and officially. In fact, let's call it:

Snarky Strategy #4

Your career goals must be *believable* and *achievable*.

We've alluded to this already, with the comments about timeframe and what's feasible to accomplish in the long-term goal horizon that the school expects. The Berkeley adcom is really, truly going to look at your goals and see if they make sense. Is this a plan that you will be able to pull off? Is it do-able? Or more like a pipe dream?

An important takeaway here is: *Don't make stuff up.* The point of this exercise is not to present the most amazing, aggressive, flamboyant-sounding goals the school has ever seen. Actually, it's usually much more effective to present goals that are very standard, traditional, perhaps even run-of-the-mill.

Bschool candidates are always told that they have to stand out, that they have to differentiate themselves. Well guess what? The career goals essay is not the place to do this.

- People are admitted to Berkeley because they have clear, rational, logical short-term goals that the Haas adcom knows they can help them achieve – *and because they are able express their own understanding of how Haas can help them do so.*

- People are admitted to Haas because they are able to show how they embody the Defining Principles. These need to be communicated through your answers to Essays 1 and 2, but they also factor in with Essay 3. If you're working too hard to impress the adcom in what you feel you'd be qualified to do post-MBA, you may come across as arrogant.

The best way to *actually* impress the Berkeley adcom (instead of *trying to* impress the adcom) is to show them that you've already built your career up to a certain point, and that you have a plan for where you want to take it from here, and you're looking for the advantage of a Berkeley MBA to do so. This means, you want to present career goals that MAKE SENSE, both given who YOU are, and given what Berkeley stands for and what they can offer to you.

If you've read the *SnarkStrategies Guide for Columbia Business School*, then you will recognize that this is similar advice to what EssaySnark provided there. But the key difference is that *Columbia and UC-Berkeley Haas are very different.*

You might be able to use the same standard career goals for both schools – and in fact you should, because you're the same person applying to both schools, so why the heck would your goals change simply because it's a different application? But you'll need to express your understanding of and appreciation for the respective schools' culture quite differently if you want to be successful at each. It's rather unusual that someone gets an offer from both Columbia and Haas unless they do their homework on each school individually and understand what they're about and demonstrate that understanding within their presentation.

Bschools are not interchangeable, regardless of how similar their career goals essay questions may sound. This is the essence of "school fit" (a term that gets bandied about in bschool admissions circles and which many people have no clue about). "School fit" is an expression of the school's culture, and the candidate's resonance with those qualities. It's a little subtle and perhaps somewhat esoteric, but it's very obvious when it's expressed appropriately in an application.

A few additional warnings:

- If you're looking to use bschool to make some **radical career change**, you have a bigger challenge. You need to show the adcom that you have transferable skills and are equipped to make the transition to the new field. This can be especially critical for those going in a dissimilar direction, e.g., IT guys wanting to go into finance. You'll need to show how you're ready to make this leap.

- Conversely, if you're not showing ENOUGH transition — if your stated **short-term goal is too similar** (or even identical) to what you are already currently doing in your job today — then you're not giving the adcom enough evidence of why you need an MBA. You should position yourself as ADVANCING, and then show how the MBA is the one main requirement that you need to get from A to B.

The Haas Essay 3 question is literally the first one we've ever seen that actually allows applicants to express how they will do all these things — yet it's the most important thing that many schools have cared about for years. We've been advising clients to pitch the schools this way for a long time because we knew that that's how the adcoms are evaluating the apps. It is refreshing, to say the least, to see an adcom finally ask the question in line with how they are evaluating you.

A Snarky Caveat

The three most common mistakes with bschool career goals are:

- **They're too vague**

- **They're too ambitious**

- **They're too broad**

If your goals suffer from any of these sins, it's highly unlikely UC-Berkeley will let you in.

- ***Too vague*** means saying you want to work in "financial services" or on an "executive team" or that you want to go into "international business." None of these are careers, they are concepts.

- ***Too ambitious*** is a goal that's written to impress the reader instead of being attainable for the candidate's actual skills and experience – often goals that involve starting a company/nonprofit/private equity fund fall into this category. It's fine to have an entrepreneurial goal, provided you lay the foundation appropriately for it.

- ***Too broad*** frequently happens when the applicant can't make up his mind and so he brings in multiple options of "I could do this or I might do that." While it could very well be true that you will pursue different options and paths once you're in the process of earning your MBA, it is usually a mistake to try and present all these different options to the adcom in their essays. There simply isn't room to provide an appropriate level of detail on more than one possible career path.

The Berkeley adcom tends to reward candidates who express (an appropriate amount of) confidence and conviction, who sound like they have an honest-to-goodness action plan. Sure, your life may take you in a different direction once the wheels are in motion. What the bschool folks want to see is that you're mature and responsible, that you know how to take control of your life and that you're able to make your own success. A well-crafted set of essays will communicate this implicitly (no, we do not recommend that you literally tell the adcom that you have done that or are that type of person).

In a nutshell: Keeping that ***realistic and believable*** guideline in mind as you refine your goals should help you avoid these problems.

One more note: Sometimes people actually make their career goals *too specific*. Usually EssaySnark is trying to cajole our clients in the opposite direction – typically their goals are not specific enough – however sometimes, we get a Brave Supplicant who takes this to an extreme. Case in point? One year we had a client state to us her long-term goal that she wants to be CMO (Chief Marketing Officer) of Apple.

Why is this a problem? Well, for starters, it implies that the Brave Supplicant thinks a little highly of herself, to assume that she's going to qualify for this cream-of-the-crop job. But the other issue: There's only one of these jobs in the whole wide world. Apple has just one CMO, and you can bet that there're a whole lotta people who'd love to be it.

You want your goals to be *achievable*, remember? Sure, you very well may end up being Chief Marketing Officer at Apple – after all, the people who go to great schools like UC-Berkeley often do end up in such high-visibility and high-impact roles. But you probably won't be there in the standard five to eight years post-MBA that the adcom has in mind with the long-term goal time horizon. And worse, you're painting yourself into a bit of a box to say that this is the one and only job you aspire to.

Instead, broaden your goal out, either by position ("a senior-level position in marketing") and/or by company ("at a leading company such as Apple or ..."). This will take you far in helping the adcom be comfortable that you're both humble, and realistic.

Essay 3: Career Goals and Why Haas

Since you've got the goals defined, and established some reasons for how you're qualified and why now is the right time, you may as well take it all the way and write the essay. This is a good one to get done first.

Let's look at the question again:

> *What is your desired post-MBA role and at what company or organization?*
>
> *a. How is your background compelling to this company?*
>
> *b. What is something you would do better for this company than any other employee?*
>
> *c. Why is an MBA necessary and how will Haas specifically help you succeed at this company?* (500-600 words inclusive)

Besides laying out literally what your goals are, you'll want to also explain why you're ready to pursue these goals (part a); that's what they're asking for with "how is your background compelling".

Then you want to *connect that background info* that you just recapped *to the goal job itself.* This is how you answer part b.

You do NOT want a part b answer that is too ethereal. No airy-fairy stuff here. No fluffbombs of insubstantial nothingness.

The way to handle part b is to use something from your past that illustrates what you bring to the table – and extrapolate from that into what the employer will gain by hiring you.

Obviously it helps to have a handle on what your intended future job is actually about. (You'd be surprised how many people seem not to.)

The most effective way to tackle parts a and b is:

- Give a very brief intro of your career to date – not simply a high-level summary of what they can see on the resume, but something extremely concise and targeted to your future. This is the foundation of your pitch.

- Then, highlight one or two specific examples that show what you have done or what your main skills or strengths are, that can be tied in to the value you expect to be able to provide at your intended post-MBA job.

Of course, the other essays should also provide some highlights from your life. But this essay needs to cover the basic qualifications for how you're prepared to pursue the goals that you're going to state with clarity and precision in this essay.

Are you stuck on that part?

OK, let's back up.

We're going to clean-slate things. We want you to mentally put aside all essay questions and career goals and other MBA ambitions, and simply look at yourself. This is an honest-to-goodness question that we're asking you to answer:

> *What's your most important attribute, skill, or key characteristic?*

What makes you tick? What makes you you? What are you most proud of? What is the major talent that you know you're great at?

Look at this from any angle at all. Make a list, even. What would your best friend identify as your #1 differentiating quality? Don't know? ASK THEM! Ask your parents, too. Do some investigation. Or think back to college: What were you known for? (Hopefully not just your proficiency at beer pong.)

The secret to doing a good job with Haas Essay 3 part b is, *it doesn't have to be a career-oriented trait that you present*. With proper insight, and a good amount of reflection, and probably many many revisions, it is very possible to write about something that seems completely un-bschool-worthy in your answer to part b, and position it in a completely appropriate way in response to this question.

Are you most proud of your double fudge brownies? Is baking your best skill set?

Great! That's an excellent starting point!

We don't advise you to say that the thing you'd do better for this intended future employer would be to bake the best brownies. Instead, we're inviting you to drill down on this skill of good-brownie-baker and look at what has *created that end state in you.*

For example: HOW DID YOU GET SO GOOD AT BAKING BROWNIES?

Was it:

- A lot of trial and error?

- Being apprenticed to a master baker – like your mom?

- Countless hours studying recipe sites on the Internet?

- Or, you grew up in a single-mom household, and you're the oldest of five kids, and because your mom worked such long hours to support all of you, you're the one who ended up having to handle stuff like bringing goodies to the class bake sale – for each of your four siblings.

Do you see where we're going with this?

Now, before you get too carried away, we are NOT trying to suggest that you can lob out a totally off-topic thing in part b and that will be sufficient. Based on the example we just provided, we can envision how some people could totally and completely eff up their entire Haas Essay 3 strategy.

What we are suggesting is that you can use the circumstances of your life – whatever they may be – as the first point of investigation, and see where that leads. This is an entry point that you can use to mine your raw material.

When you're trying to come up with an honest way to answer a question like this, then you can think of it like unraveling a blanket: You look for a loose thread, and when you find one, you tug on it, and see how far it goes.

When you make lists, or you pose a question to yourself – "Self? What is true for you about *this?*" – then you are like a detective doing some investigative work. You become alert and you look for clues. You scan the horizon. You see what comes up.

Your subconscious knows some EXCELLENT reasons for what you could do at your intended future job that's better than what anyone else could do. Put forth some effort in mining that subconscious and you will be surprised at what it may summon forth for you.

A Snarky Caveat

Avoid grandiose statements in your answer to part b.

What we mean by that is, you need to base your part b answer on something that you can prove. Tie it into something from your past – either through a connection to the background information that you're providing in the part a answer, or by a specific reference that you include in your part b section.

This is evidence-based essay-writing, and it's the most effective way to go.

How do you handle it if you want to be an entrepreneur?

This situation may actually be even easier for you than it is for someone with a more traditional goal. If you have the ~~audacity~~ courage and conviction to pitch the adcom with an entrepreneurial goal, then what a great opportunity this is to show them how this is the right future for you. It's very important for someone coming in with an entrepreneurial vision to establish how they have some foundational experiences, mindset, knowledge, or skills to make that idea a reality. Just spouting off about your interest in being an entrepreneur is totally not enough. You don't want the essay to turn into a business plan – the focus needs to stay on YOU and your skills – but this part of the essay question is a great way to convey to the adcom how you're uniquely qualified to pursue it.

It also forces you to put some rubber to the road. This will help weed out many of the people who are very casual in their entrepreneurial aspirations. In a way, Haas's career goals essay is serving as a self-validation test for you: If you can't sufficiently answer the part b question, then are you really ready for this thing you say you want to do?

It reminds us a little bit of this situation with Steve Blank's very popular entrepreneurship class – we're not sure if this incident happened at Berkeley, or at some other school where he teaches, but it communicates absolutely the same type of thing that this Essay 3 part b thing will screen for: commitment is important.

http://blogs.berkeley.edu/2014/02/06/sometimes-it-pays-to-be-a-jerk/

This Haas career goals question may deter more BSers from being too flamboyant in their career goals essays. You don't want this essay to diverge into a business plan describing your intended company. Instead, you need to focus on why you're the right person to pursue the business. The adcom won't be trying to rip apart your idea, in terms of whether there's a market for it or what the competitive landscape looks like or any of that (unless the idea is patently ridiculous on its surface). Instead, they'll be looking to see if you have the requisite industry experience, including potentially the right connections, and definitely an understanding of the sector, such that you will be a force to be reckoned with when you go out to do this thing.

That's how you can leverage part b of this essay to your advantage as a wanna-be entrepreneur: Write your answer to show how you're the best person in the world to pursue this opportunity, based on specific references or examples of what you'll draw on and what you bring to bear as an advantage.

Also just a final comment: It's always easier for an adcom to be convinced by an entrepreneurial goal if the BSer has already begun it. If you can point to efforts expanded and progress made to date, then you're upping the odds that they'll be able to buy into this idea.

Just be aware that there's a slight risk with someone who has a going venture already and is saying they want to go to bschool: The adcom will want to know what you plan to do with the business while you're in school. It's unrealistic to think that any "real" business can be managed on the side while you're simultaneously pursuing a full-time MBA program. If that's your situation, then the adcom is likely going to see you as a likely better fit to the EWMBA. If you're dog-determined to go for full-time instead, then this is the place where you need to express the reasons why.

Next up for advice on how to map out your Haas goals essay is how to allocate your 600 words.

How to structure Haas Essay 3

We can see how this essay might end up being five neat paragraphs on the page. Here's the way that we would write it, if we were applying to Haas – along with our view on how much space you should devote to each section of content.

- *INTRO - Paragraph 1:* What is your goal? Short and sweet should suffice just fine (15% of your word count)

- *Paragraph 2:* Why are you ready to pursue this? Give us some context, establish a foundation, share a bit of backstory – with everything pointing towards the goal you named in paragraph 1. (30% of words)

- *Paragraph 3:* What's special about you? Otherwise known as, what unique contribution can you make, and/or why would that company want to hire you? This can be an extension of the background info provided in paragraph 2 (or at least, it should not contradict it in any way). This doesn't have to literally be a hard skill that you "do better" than anyone else; you can go deeper than that. (30%)

- *Paragraph 4:* Why do you need an MBA to do this, and why do you want to go to Haas to get it? (20%)

- *Conclusion:* A sentence or two to wrap everything up. (5%)

They've structured the essay prompt with the individual sub-questions in order to guide you in how to structure your response, however you should *not* write separate answers to the separate a, b, and c sections. Your essay should be smooth, and complete, with a formal introduction, fluid transitions between each major idea or section, and a conclusion that wraps everything up at the end.

In terms of length: Because this is a longer essay, you should be able to convey what you need within the limit provided by the adcom. You can go over 600 words – they don't count words in your submitted essays – but you shouldn't go bonkers with it. This is already on the longer side, where bschool admissions essays are concerned. A 630-ish word essay is probably fine; anything over 700 words, gosh, definitely not.

Snarky Strategy #5

Even though we have asserted that part c is the most important piece of the essay, it should get the fewest words allocated.

This is a loose recommendation and if you need to take the essay in a different direction that changes the overall balance, it may be absolutely fine. But from the Haas adcom perspective, *what* you want to do, and *why* you are qualified are both pretty darn important.

The beginning is also important, and we actually don't recommend you get too creative there. As stiff and unimaginative as it may seem, we strongly recommend that you start the Haas essay by simply answering the question. "After I graduate with my MBA from Haas, I intend to..." Obviously you can (and should) use your own language to say it. Having the actual literal black-and-white answer to the question right at the beginning, in the opening line (or at minimum opening paragraph) makes your job in communicating those goals to the reader so much simpler.

Because, uh, you have to communicate the goals. Since that's what the whole essay is supposed to be about – and because you have so much other stuff you need to jam into this essay related to the goals – then it would be awesome to give the reader the answer to the question right away. Why make her wait?

That's not the only way you can do it, but it's a straightforward way, and it usually works.

The Berkeley career goals question has a similar angle to what NYU and Columbia also ask: "Why do you need an MBA **now**???" NYU asks you to speak to your goals from "this point in your life", while Columbia's question starts off with "given your individual background." In all of these cases, it helps tremendously if you give the adcom a snapshot of the elements of your career, and/or your life, that are specifically relevant to your intended future goals. Many bschools don't ask anything about the past in their career goals question. Haas wants to know why you're capable and qualified to pursue this great thing you're laying out for yourself, based on who you are today, and why is now the right time.

Another big component to the Haas essay is, they want to see how you approach the question itself. They want to make sure you can read and follow directions. They care about how you break down the problem of developing your essay, and how you construct your thoughts in response to the questions they've asked. What you say definitely matters, and how you say it is also very important.

Since we're talking about "breaking stuff down": We do not recommend answering this question in a three-part essay. Make it one cohesive argument that answers the questions in an integrated fashion.

A Snarky Caveat

Be sure to literally answer each sub-part!

Too often, a Brave Supplicant writes – and writes and writes and writes – and ends up with a draft, and they submit it for review (or even worse, submit it with their app) – yet despite the fact that they went well past the adcom's suggested word count, they failed to answer the question. You can write a lot and still completely miss the mark.

The best way to assure that you have a firm and clear response to each of the four questions they're asking (yes there are 4, even though there are only 3 subparts) is to *print out your draft and take a red pen to it.* Reach each part of the essay question, one at a time, and literally underline where in the essay you answered it.

Each answer should be a sentence or two at the max. You're looking for the part where you have a direct and specific response to what was queried. Sometimes people feel that half the essay is being responsive to the prompt, but the 'half' that they point to is just a jumble of ideas, without a direct answer literally to the question.

Your reader should not have to hunt for the answers – nor should they ever wonder if this essay was originally written for another school. It should be patently obvious, on the face of things, that this is a Haas essay. The adcom should be able to pick out what you have intended as your response to each part of the question.

And no, you should not use subheadings.

Not only do we think that they are clunky – they turn an essay into a report – but they also are unnecessary. They are cheap devices. You shouldn't need to tell the reader what you're answering, by using a title on that section; the answer itself should answer it. Also, subheadings take away from your already-limited word count, and they create unnecessary space on the page, so why use them?

Wow, EssaySnark said a lot about the career goals. They're important – but so is everything else about this essay. Essay 3 is where you impart your love for Haas. This is where you pull out all the stops and talk with enthusiasm about what you know about Berkeley, and why those attributes are important to you.

This is where:

- You impress the adcom with all the efforts you've made to research the program, reach out to the students and alumni, interact with the admissions team, and engage with the Haas community – including, ideally, your visit to campus
- You articulate your understanding for what Berkeley is about in a way that shows how you will leverage same in your own educational process

This essay should talk about *specifics*. With this question, the Haas adcom is encouraging you to come to campus, or to meet the admissions team as they travel the world. They used to have a question that asked how you had gotten to know them. This stuff matters to them. Do some networking, ask some questions. Take the time to find out if Haas is really the right place for you, and then reflect on the reasons why – and put THAT in this essay.

A Snarky Caveat

If you visited campus or attended an info session – *tell them about it!* **Include the month of your interaction in Essay 3 (include the year, too, if it was not recent). Name some names.**

The way to make a strong pitch to Haas or any school is to include specifics in your arguments. Nowhere is this more important than in your Berkeley career goals essay.

Haas Essay 3 is a critically important part of your application. Plan for significant time to map out your strategy, and even more time to rewrite your draft. Don't rush this one. Good writing requires effort, and that effort takes time. Be prepared for a full process of revision and rework to make your essay shine.

Your Two Supporting Essays

Moving on.

Before you tackle your other Haas essays, you should complete two exercises:

1. Make sure you understand the Defining Principles (by this time, you should be able to recite them from memory).

2. Develop a list of your own accomplishments and failures to pull potential essay topics from.

We've already told you a bunch of times how to learn about Haas and its culture, so you should have that first part nailed. To prove to yourself that you really do have it nailed, you might want to take four blank sheets of paper and across the top of each, write one of the Defining Principles. Then, without looking on the Internet, see if you can write for yourself what each one of those Principles means. In your own words. Your interpretation.

Having a full understanding of these Principles will help you identify what stories to use in your essays, and will also help you when you go to interview with Haas.

On the second exercise, we'll give you more explicit instructions. Here's the assignment we give new clients when we're starting out on an admissions consulting engagement with them.

EssaySnark's brainstorming exercise for new clients

[Based on the actual email we send out.]

> As another step in developing your application theme, a useful exercise is to brainstorm about your major accomplishments. Haas wants to learn about you through your achievements and what you've done in your life. Where you've focused your energies and attention, and the impact you've had in the world (even on a small stage), will communicate volumes to the adcom. Getting an "inventory" of your major wins and significant life experiences will give you a sense of what to work from in creating your strategy.
>
> Put together a simple list of, say, your five (or six, or seven) most important achievements.
>
> **It's not recommended to write full essays for the purpose of this exercise.** This is about getting some ideas down, not in starting to write the actual essays. People often get attached to a draft if they write it all out; it can be hard to redirect and start over. If you start to write a lot about one achievement, then stop. For the purpose of this exercise, it's best to just capture your key ideas. Make a list, that's all we're looking for. Since this is just for you, a bunch of backstory or explanation is not needed. That can come later, as you flesh the ideas out to a real essay. For now, just get the gist of each one; you shouldn't have to dig through a bunch of words to find the core of the achievement or event.
>
> These achievements can be taken from literally any area of your life — the classroom, team projects, internships, community engagement with volunteering, extracurriculars from school, sports, even personal things like overcoming illness or dealing with parents' divorce or whatever. Lay it all out on a piece of paper. Anything is fair game at this stage. You should not edit yourself in terms of where these items come from in your life, nor need you worry about how current or ancient history they might be. When you go to create your essays, you'll mostly want to cover what you've done in the past three or four years, but for the purposes of this exercise, you can include anything at all of importance to you.
>
> Where were the pivot-points in your life? Where did the track diverge and you started moving in a new direction?
>
> Where did people stand up and applaud at something awesome that you did?

What does your mother brag to her friends about?

When thinking of professional accomplishments, try to identify ones where you met a tangible goal ("completed a project two weeks early", "passed an industry exam and received a professional certification", etc.), or specifically, achievements where your efforts made a direct contribution to your team, the customer, or the overall company in ways that can be measured ("reduced costs by 10%", "made the customer so happy that they bought another $100k product from us", etc.).

Here's a video from a few years back by Darden's Director of Admissions with a great idea on how to identify some of these more recent pivotal experiences or moments:

http://www.youtube.com/watch?v=dujl_GT6Uxo

Finally, if you're stuck on this: Force yourself to come up with ideas by doing a timed writing exercise. The way it works is this:

1. Set yourself up in a quiet place with a pen and a notepad.

2. At the top of the page, write in big block letters: MY MOST SIGNIFICANT ACCOMPLISHMENTS ARE.

3. Get a kitchen timer. Set it for five minutes.

4. Put the pen on the paper and start writing — and don't let yourself stop.

Keep that pen moving until the timer goes off. It doesn't matter if you're writing about the topic at first — you could even begin by writing "I have no idea what to write." Just force yourself to write, don't worry about punctuation and spelling, nobody's going to see it. Keep going for the entire five minutes. Don't let the pen stop moving on the page.

Nothing come of it? Give yourself a minute, get a cup of coffee, sit back down and do it again. Maybe change the prompt at the top of the page this time: WHAT AM I MOST PROUD OF? or WHERE HAVE I HAD AN IMPACT ON OTHERS?

You may feel a little silly doing this exercise, but people are often surprised at what comes up — it's a way to force the subconscious mind into action, and sometimes it spits up some real gems!

So that's the second step: Creating a list. (Or two, actually.) You may not find all the material for the first three essay questions among these lists of achievements and failures, however it's likely that you will find most of it.

Go through the lists and tag each item that you came up with based on the four Defining Principles. You know the ones, *Confidence without Attitude*, *Student Always*, etc. See if you can identify which (if any) of these Haas Principles is reflected by or in evidence within each of the stories you've got down. Don't force it; it's possible that some stories don't have anything to do with any of the Principles. And, some stories may actually demonstrate or reflect more than one of them. Take a gander through your background with this lens and see what you discover.

As you select your topics, keep in mind what your career goals are and how you can highlight for the reader the transferable skills and/or relevant experience you've had that will set you up for success in this new career. Think as well about what personal qualities you can showcase (reflect on those Defining Principles to see where you can give them those angles).

A little break for encouragement

We wanted to share an email we received from a Brave Supplicant in early January of 2014:

```
Hey guys, I am very very happy to inform you that I
got the call from Haas last Friday and I'm in!!! I
still feel like floating, it's been an amazing
weekend and ... well, you know how people feel at
this point very well :-) Although I did not use the
decimator service for this one, the Haas Guide was a
wonderful tool to work my app, so somehow I partly
owe it to you. Thank you!
```

This is a different BSer than the one we quoted on the front cover.

So there you have it: Two examples that prove you can do this!! Let's keep going.

How to think about these essays

Each of the three Haas essays are actually quite similar, in that these are all opportunities for you to share your awesomeness with the adcom, to communicate to them who you are and how you're different and why you're a good fit for the Berkeley-Haas School of Business. The main thing to focus on is *use details to communicate your point.* The essays should each have a clear and direct answer to the specific question (or subpart) and you need to find examples as backup to those answers.

To (over)simplify your approach:

- Essay 1 should consist of a single story that includes a beginning, a middle, and an end, with a DIRECT ANSWER to the "how did this transform you?" question (typically stated either in the conclusion, or alternatively presented as part of the intro).

- Essay 2 should also be a story that clearly depicts *what you did* with enough context to convey either implicitly or through a direct answer to the unasked question of "why was it significant?' *why it was significant* – to your teammates, the organization, the client, or even to yourself. You must "show" the reader why it was significant, and you must keep the focus on your actions to do that.

When we say "story" we mean something from your life that illustrates the point that you're making. Obviously in the first question about an experience that changed you, they are asking for a literal description of a specific episode when something like that occurred to you.

This is key. So much so, that we'll emphasize it as

Snarky Strategy #6

Essay 1 should each be a DIRECT ANSWER supported by a story. Essay 2 should be a STORY that easily answers the unasked question of "why is this significant?"

Of course, we're not going to leave it at that. Here are some further guidelines to use as you evaluate which of your amazing stories to include in these essays.

Personal or professional content?

- Personal stories are better, usually, as the basis for your answer for Essay 1. Sometimes when people use a professional story for Essay 1, it seems a little contrived, like they're trying to say what they think they're supposed to say. Most people have the most transformational experiences in their lives happen outside of work. If you want to use a work-based story for Essay 1, then the change in your worldview must be very easy for your reader to understand.

This might be something about a personal challenge, or a crisis, dilemma, or setback, such as being laid off, a health issue, losing a parent, an accident, or possibly a story about significant weight loss or other personal triumph. This is not mandatory, but sharing something personal with the adcom (done in an appropriate, professional, and relevant way) can illuminate elements of your background for them and help them see who you are. Be careful not to go into TMI territory though! (See the EssaySnark blahg at http://essaysnark.com/2010/11/tmi-or-not-tmi-more-on-evaluating.html for some guidance on what might be considered "TMI" in bschool essays.)

- Essay 2 must be professional in nature, based on how they asked the question – and remember, most of your content if not all for Essay 3 needs to be professional, too, with a couple soundbite highlights from your career to back up your career goals. Combined, all content of these Haas essays should be weighted towards professional stories.

- It's hopefully obvious but just for the record: A "professional" story could include any work-related achievement that happened on the job or that was related to your career. The best stories of accomplishment show a *contribution* or in some other way are able to demonstrate impact. There should be a "before" and an "after" state apparent from the story: You were faced with a specific challenge or problem to solve, you did XYZ, and then the outcomes were this. There's other ways to do it, but that template usually communicates what you need to communicate. If you're coming out of college or another academic program, academic achievements would also count as "professional" stories (though as already noted, Berkeley is not too keen on candidates without significant work experience).

- If your quantitative skills are not self-evident through the other parts of your application – in other words, if you scored lower than a 46 or so on the quant side of the GMAT, or if you ever had a C or worse in a quant subject in college, and if you're not working in an obviously analytical field – then one way to counter that is to feature one story that has a quant edge to it. If you can find a way to highlight a professional project where you built a model, developed the budget, or even ran some type of analytics on something, then that can add value – but please don't choose such a story only because it's got a quant edge, if it's not the strongest story to offer. If you can expound on those quant skills, then the example must be specific in terms of how you describe what you did. When done right, this type of multi-dimensional approach can add a lot of value for the adcom in understanding your capabilities in a limited amount of essay real estate.

- It is not necessary to cover extracurriculars in your Haas essays. You have an entire section of the app, in the Supplemental Information, to log this stuff, and it should also be on your resume. If you have an important experience to relate in Essay 1 that comes from the domain of your community service activities or team sports, then great – but it's not necessary. Travel and marathons are pretty typical topics for bschool essays, so hopefully you have something exceedingly important to discuss if you're going to use a story in either of those categories.

- You should be able to clearly identify traces of at least one, preferably two, of the Defining Principles in the stories you tell in these essays. It is not necessary to have each of the Principles reflected; in fact that's probably impossible with the shorter essays and fewer numbers of them in the current app. However, your task is to highlight how you fit into the Haas culture through the stories you choose, and so you should work hard to present examples from your life where you embody these traits. You should not need to explicitly state the Defining Principle in your answer; it should be apparent from the story that you relate. That's the essence of the advice to "show, don't tell" in your essays – which can rather dramatically backfire if you say something like, "And that's how I proved to everybody that I am confident without attitude." Uh, right.

- Finally, *be honest*. Last year, Haas asked applicants to identify a song that they feel reflected who they are. Most people tried to say something that sounds good; they came up with a song that's so damned cliched – like U2's *Beautiful Day*. Do you know how many people used that song in that essay?? You can do better than that. These essays require you to go deeper. On essay 1 in particular, you have a chance to show the kind of person you are today. What makes you tick? Who *are* you? The adcom wants to know that. And the best way you can share who you are with them is a) answer the question directly; and b) provide an example or a quick story to illustrate how it is true. This is what winning essays are made of. You can do this, Brave Supplicant!

We'll dive into that here in a brief second, but first let's wrap up these macro comments on essays 1 and 2 with this:

A Snarky Caveat

**Do not repeat stories between the different essays!
Come up with unique material
to present in each one.**

Even in the longer career goals essay where you're supposed to show how you're ready for the MBA, you should not duplicate examples or stories that you've used in the other essays. Everything you present across these essays is a chance to highlight something new or different about your background and profile. You can, and almost always should, have those same examples on the resume, and in some cases it might make sense for a recommender to mention the stuff you're talking about in the essays. The allocation of content across the entirety of your application should be reviewed carefully.

Essay 1: Your Transformation

EssaySnark thinks this is a great question:

> *Describe an experience that has fundamentally changed the way you see the world. How did this transform you?* (400-500 words)

The trick here? In order to show how you've been "transformed", we must see a "before" picture. Or in some other way, you need to do a compare-and-contrast. "I was one way, then this happened, and I realized X." Be sure to include some way for the reader to see what you were like previous to this, in order to appreciate how it changed you.

And, remember that the best way to demonstrate change is through actions. How did you act differently as a result of this transformation? There might be other ways to depict "transformation" but merely stating that you were transformed is hardly compelling.

This essay typically works best when you use a story about something *that happened to you* where there were external events acting on you as a being in this world. You need to quickly describe what the "thing" was that happened, but then the bulk of the essay should be about what you did in response (actions are important), with some reflection at the end on the meaning of it all.

Also, try to show how you acted differently in a subsequent situation because of this experience you had.

Something like, "I went through layoffs, and it made me appreciate how important it is to my self esteem to be gainfully employed, and then six months ago at my new company I had a chance to mentor someone who was at risk to be terminated due to performance." That's a really clumsy example that we made up in five seconds, and it isn't very impressive by any means, so please don't think that that's a template to use. We're offering it only to communicate the basic structure of how to do this.

A 500-word essay is plenty to cover all those points. Heck, you might be able to do it in 400 words. Most important is to share an experience where it's obvious why it had an impact on you – and if it's not obvious, then you need to explain it, though that's certainly not the ideal strategy of execution here. The insights you share on the transformation are just as important, and the very best way that you can demonstrate you really were transformed is in how you talk about the actions you took subsequent to the experience.

Extra special brownie points if your "transformation" fits in with the Defining Principles. (It should NOT show you as a complete jerk in the beginning and now you're different; please don't use as a "before" state an example where you had "confidence WITH attitude" or something like that. We'd be nervous about the execution of such an essay.)

This essay is where we can see who you are as a person. Telling a story is how you come across as authentic, and three-dimensional.

Should you use a failure story for essay 1?

For many years, Haas has asked applicants to write an essay about a failure. Those are always fun to read! That type of story might sometimes work well for essay 1. Typically it's the failures and setbacks in life that prove to be our greatest teachers, right? So this is another area you can mine for possible ideas.

If you do use a failure story – where you personally were the one who royally screwed something up – then you need to do more to tell what happened than you might otherwise if you were just talking about an event that happened to you. You will need to show the reader what you did to cause the screw-up, and then what you learned from it. And somewhere along the way in that essay, you need to show how you fixed it.

If you screwed everything up on the project and it was a total shambles – great! That definitely qualifies as a "failure" story to use for this essay! But you can't leave the reader with the impression of shambles in her head. You need to show how you became a clean-up crew, how you morphed into Superman and saved the day. You need to show how you totally rectified the situation and redeemed yourself. And ideally you'll also mention a subsequent project or circumstance where you were faced with a similar problem and you didn't repeat the past behaviors but instead took a totally different tack and came out a winner straight through. Yes, it's hard to do all that in the confines of such a small essay, but it's possible. And you may be in a good position to reveal some interesting stuff about yourself.

Just one idea to consider. It's not necessary to bare your soul of your darkest mistakes. Lots of stories might be contenders for this essay.

The adcoms do appreciate when someone is real.

Essay 2: Most Significant Professional Accomplishment

This is practically a permanent part of the Haas essay collection – except that this year, they changed it so that you must use a professional story. Which makes sense. It's an application to a professional program, so getting more evidence of how you're qualified and ready for that is helpful for them in evaluating you.

Here's what they want to know:

> *What is your most significant professional accomplishment?*
> (200-300 words)

Harvard asked a question like this for years and years, and it's been on the Haas application for awhile too. Why? Because it's a great opportunity for you to share more of who you are (there that phrase is again) while also potentially letting you shine as a leader.

You'll notice that there's no timeframe requirement for this one. They want you to give the thing that really is the "most significant." Don't use something that you think they want you to talk about; use the one that is most meaningful to you. And then, explain why.

That being said – even though there literally is no time requirement on this one – if you go *too* far back in your life, the adcom may wonder why you don't have something more recent to present. You're supposed to be showing how you're an overachiever who's ahead of his peers. If you haven't done anything significant in like the last five years, well, that's sort of a possible red flag. If the thing you want to present is dated but it's REALLY an extreme accomplishment, then we can go along with that – or, if you have a REALLY good reason for why and how it's so significant, then perhaps that's OK too. Anything not really current needs to be GOOD.

Just don't make it *too* recent or we're worried in another direction. Typically the things that are the most significant are ones that need some time to build, and ferment, and then pop. It's rare that you would achieve something really big just yesterday and be able to talk today about its great significance in your life. Usually a big achievement needs some time to cure, and some distance before its meaning is felt. A little bit off in the dust of your life is fine, and maybe preferable, for the story you use in this essay. This isn't a rule, just a suggestion, based on what we've seen from other people.

Also note that they asked for ONE. You cannot present multiple accomplishments in this essay. You won't have room to do that, and anyway, it's literally not what they have asked for.

The main litmus test for which accomplishment you choose: **It needs to be something that you personally took action to achieve.** It's fine and great if it was a team-based effort, but it needs to be YOUR accomplishment, that you worked towards, that you pulled off. Your contribution needs to be the focus of how you present the story.

If you can fit in an explanation in the opening or closing paragraph about why you chose this specific thing to present, that might be a nice touch too — although honestly, as already stated, it should be self-evident. It should be obvious to any reader why this is the most important thing in your life that you're presenting.

Before you get too far with essays 1 and 2

Now that you have ideas for both essays, you need to take a step back. You need to examine your strategy.

After you've picked your accomplishment and transformation story — before you start writing the essays — step back and ask yourself, *What do I want the takeaway message to be?*

What are you trying to communicate about yourself with these two examples from your life?

What do you want the adcom to know about you as a result of this combination of stories?

You should be able to extract a specific word or two about each one, an adjective that is the key idea of each. Add them up. Are these qualities that you think make you into a top-tier MBA candidate?

Earlier we mentioned a basic list of qualities that Haas cares about (see page 14). Are you demonstrating any of these in your essays?

If someone knows just these few facts about you — that you accomplished this thing on the one hand, and that you had this experience that changed you on the other, what is the net-net? What do you think a complete stranger would assume to be true about the type of person you are, based on just those facts?

Now look at your answer to essay 3, on the "why MBA" question. Do the takeaway messages of these facts support your pitch of why you want an MBA? And why you deserve to be at Haas based on what you've done and the kind of person you are?

You may need to tweak the messaging a little — or a lot — before you find the right mix.

So there you have it, Brave Supplicant. A map to guide you through the career goals essay, and the two supporting essays for Haas. This should keep you plenty busy for awhile!

Interviewing

Interviews are required for admission to Berkeley, but that doesn't mean that all candidates are interviewed. Instead, interviews are by invitation only. Invites begin going out about a month after the deadline, all the way up to the decision date. The timing of when your invitation comes through has nothing to do with the strength of your candidacy. Still, the wait for the invite to appear in your inbox can be excruciating.

Berkeley typically invites around 25-30% of their candidates to the full-time program to interview; they invite about two-thirds of EWMBA candidates. They generally extend an offer to about half of the candidates, respectively.

To put real numbers behind that:

- In the 2012-2013 admissions season (the last numbers available as of this writing), Haas accepted something like 480 applicants to their full-time program, out of 3,422 apps submitted.

- Their alumni conducted about 800 interviews; probably another 100 interviews were done on campus by current students and staff.

The EWMBA program interviews candidates themselves; in other words, the admissions team does those interviews, and they also sometimes invite candidates to interview even before they've submitted their application. If you've registered in their admissions portal, then they may contact you with an invitation to interview around an information session scheduled in your area – for example, if you live in Orange County, and they're doing an EWMBA info session in LA, you might get an invitation to interview at that time.

The full-time program primarily relies on alumni to conduct interviews in the applicant's city. It is not necessary to travel to campus to interview (but you could).

If you're invited to interview for the full-time program, they ask that you submit official copies of your transcripts at that time. Unofficial copies may be uploaded into the online application at time of submit but they need the official ones before they can render a final decision. If you anticipate that it will take some time for your undergraduate institution to send over official versions, you may want to request them to be sent to you in advance; just don't have them mailed to Berkeley until they ask for them.

We can't wait to hear that you've been invited to interview! Hopefully you make it to that stage and then sail straight in with an admit. Good luck to you!

What to Do Next

So you've read through this whole guide and you should know what to do. Before you launch into your crafting and drafting process, take a moment to answre these questions:

- Can you recite the four Defining Principles now?
- Can you offer an example from your own life that illustrates at least one or two? Great. If not, you know what to do.

Next, we've already told you about how helpful it would be to visit Haas. We'll say it again, in case you didn't believe us the first time. GO VISIT HAAS. Check out the campus. Explore the city of Berkeley. Both are different (!) places (in all meanings of the word!). Make sure you know why this is the place for you.

You should also do additional firsthand research, like checking out the professors, learning which amazing people in the world are alumni, reading up on them. And of course, you need to work on those essays.

This should be plenty obvious, but we'll state it anyway: You will likely find that multiple revisions on your Berkeley essays will be of benefit. These essays are going to be a lot of work for you. It's unlikely that you'll be successful in your bid for Berkeley if you don't leave yourself ample time to work on them – both in terms of blocks of time to write up your drafts, as well as calendar time to work through the creative process required in generating a good essay. You're also going to need time to construct your Dean's Fellowship essay – we're presuming you're going to get an offer from Haas and so that is the next step (yes, another essay!!). We offer an online-only Haas Scholarship Essay strategy guidelette thingie on our site, available in the EssaySnark bookstore.

Good luck with the Berkeley app, Brave Supplicant!

EssaySnark reviews essays for the top business schools on our blahg (for free!) at http://essaysnark.com. We've got lots of material in articles and Q&A about Berkeley there. If you have questions we can help with about Haas or any of your other applications, feel free to email us at gethelpnow@essaysnark.com or find us on Twitter (@EssaySnark).

Look for other *SnarkStrategies Guides* (digital and paperback) at your favorite bookseller or on the EssaySnark blahg.

FOLLOW ESSAYSNARK ON TWITTER!

> "We have been brought up personally to have social responsibilities."
>
> WALTER A. HAAS

www.ingramcontent.com/pod-product-compliance
Lightning Source LLC
Chambersburg PA
CBHW080527110426
42742CB00017B/3260